Easter Mysteries

John O'Boyle

Easter Mysteries

Participant Guide to the Film with Leader Helps

by Mike Poteet

Abingdon Press
Nashville

EASTER MYSTERIES
PARTICIPANT GUIDE TO THE FILM WITH LEADER HELPS

Copyright © 2020 Abingdon Press
All rights reserved.

No part of this work may be reproduced or transmitted in any form or by any means, electronic or mechanical, including photocopying and recording, or by any information storage or retrieval system, except as may be expressly permitted by the 1976 Copyright Act or in writing from the publisher. Requests for permission can be addressed to Permissions, The United Methodist Publishing House, 2222 Rosa L. Parks Blvd., Nashville, TN, 37228-1306 or e-mailed to permissions@umpublishing.org.

Library of Congress Control Number: 2019950853
ISBN 978-1-5018-9972-0

Scripture quotations unless noted otherwise are taken from the Common English Bible, copyright 2011. Used by permission. All rights reserved.

Scripture quotations marked NRSV are from the New Revised Standard Version Bible, copyright © 1989 National Council of the Churches of Christ in the United States of America. Used by permission. All rights reserved worldwide. http://nrsvbibles.org/

20 21 22 23 24 25 26 27 28 29—10 9 8 7 6 5 4 3 2 1
MANUFACTURED IN THE UNITED STATES OF AMERICA

The Cast

Wallace Smith
as Jesus

Erin Davie
as Mary Magdalene

Kevin Earley
as Peter

P. J. Griffith
as Judas

Phillip Boykin
as Caiaphas

Michael X. Martin
as Pilate

Stephen Lee Anderson
as Herod

Benjamin Howes
as Thomas

Ruth Gottschall
as Miriam

Bronson Norris Murphy
as Andrew

J. D. Webster
as Simon

The Cast

Steffanie Leigh
as Naomi

Anna Mintzer
as Joanna

Jason Simon
as Cleopas

Paul Lessard
as John

Kent Overshown
as Centurion

Lucy Horton
as Vox Angeli

Sumayya Ali
Ensemble

Joy Hermalyn
Ensemble

Taylor Coriell
Ensemble

Joanne Javien
Ensemble

Ariela Morgenstern
Ensemble

Contents

Foreword 9

Preface 19

Session 1: Passion 25

Session 2: Resurrection 45

Session 3: Mission 61

Leader Helps 83

Notes 91

Foreword

Mike Poteet

Passion Plays—Powerful and Problematic

The events of Jesus's last week on earth—his arrival in Jerusalem and his cleansing of the Temple there; the meal he shared with his disciples; his arrest, trials, and crucifixion; followed by the discovery of his empty tomb and his resurrection appearances—are some of the most dramatic events in the Gospels. Naturally, then, playwrights, composers, performers, and other artists have wanted for centuries to bring these events to life on stage.

The church's rituals contained the seeds of such dramas, especially the Eucharist with its rehearsal of Jesus's commandment to remember him in the sharing of bread and wine, and the Good Friday liturgy, which featured priests and congregation reading or chanting the account of his Passion found in the Gospel of John.

In Europe, during the Middle Ages, these liturgical "dramas" moved out of the church building as popular and (to varying degrees) pious forms of entertainment. Passion plays dramatized Jesus's suffering and death, often in elaborate and extrabiblical detail. They also frequently fanned the flames of anti-Jewish sentiment by presenting Jewish characters—other than Jesus and his disciples, whose identities as devout Jews were downplayed or ignored—as wicked, even demonic villains.

Because Passion plays translate Scripture into live action, they have been and can still be powerful experiences for many theatergoers. The perennially popular, oft-revived *Jesus Christ Superstar* (1970) and *Godspell* (1971), for example, are "Passion plays" in the musical theater mode, and appeal to wide audiences of Christians and non-Christians alike. The historic Oberammergau Passion Play in Germany, first mounted in 1634 and produced almost every decade since, will see its forty-second production in 2020, drawing crowds from around the world.

But Passion plays' historic problems can still plague them. In 1930, for instance, Adolf Hitler praised the Oberammergau play for "convincingly" portraying "the menace of Jewry."[1] (The Oberammergau play has been significantly revised in recent years to avoid anti-Semitism, and to highlight Jesus's Jewish faith.[2]) In 2004, director Mel Gibson's *The Passion of the Christ* drew criticism for repeating old anti-Jewish stereotypes as well as for dramatizing Jesus's suffering and death with abundant blood and brutality. Sister Rose Pacatte of the *National Catholic Reporter* went so far as to review Gibson's *Passion* as a horror film.[3]

Foreword

Easter Mysteries—A Passion Play for the Twenty-First Century

Tony Award–winning Broadway producer John O'Boyle wrote *Easter Mysteries* to continue the Passion play tradition by taking it in a new direction. (In fact, *The New Passion Play* was one of its early titles!) He wanted to not only dramatize the story of Jesus's death without anti-Jewish elements but also emphasize what followed Jesus's Passion more than the Passion itself.

In a video interview released in 2016, O'Boyle contrasts his work with other modern musical Passion plays: "If you look at the cultural Easter stories like *Jesus Christ Superstar* and *Godspell*, they stop at the Crucifixion. And actually, I think it's the time after the Crucifixion, and how the disciples learned of the Resurrection and embraced it that's fascinating and interesting."[4]

Easter Mysteries began its life as a one-act Palm Sunday musical O'Boyle wrote for the congregation he belonged to, St. Martin's in-the-Field Episcopal Church in Severna Park, Maryland.[5] "That production," he recalls in an interview with film critic Nell Minow, "which ended right after the crucifixion, took on a life of its own and was repeated as a fundraiser, invited to a large clergy conference, and then invited to and performed in an 11th-century Norman church in Swansea, Wales."[6] Later, O'Boyle wrote a second, separate one-act work titled *Quem*

Quaeritis that continued the story through Jesus's ascension. It was staged in Severna Park and at the Episcopal Cathedral in Baltimore.

In 2013, O'Boyle combined "extensively rewritten" versions of both pieces to create *Easter Mysteries*. The complete work debuted at St. Clement's Episcopal Church in New York City. It was ultimately filmed and screened in movie theaters on March 22, 2016. It aired on ABC in the spring of 2017, and on NBC on Easter Sunday of 2018.

Inviting Everyone into the Great Mystery of Faith

During the Eucharist in many Christian traditions (also called Holy Communion or the Lord's Supper), worshippers recite or sing the "great mystery of faith": "Christ has died, Christ is risen, Christ will come again." It is the Christian community's primary proclamation. As the apostle Paul writes, it is "the good news" passed on from generation to generation "as most important" (**1 Corinthians 15:1, 3**).

Easter Mysteries tells the story behind this statement of faith. As theology professor Philip Cunningham told Religion News Service, O'Boyle's work "is less concerned with the causes or the extent of [Jesus's] sufferings than with the new life that Christians find in the Raised Jesus."[7]

But *Easter Mysteries* is not solely for Christian audiences. It seeks to speak to all people by presenting its protagonists—Peter, Mary Magdalene, John, Judas, and others—as ordinary people in whom audience members can see themselves. O'Boyle explains: "I had set out to write a Passion Play that de-iconized these characters. They seem to appear in a lot of holy art and so on as very all-knowing, aware of everything that's going to happen, and so forth. I think for people like me, that's a hard thing to relate to."[8]

One way *Easter Mysteries* re-humanizes the Easter story's characters is in its deliberately diverse cast. "We wanted the cast to look like America," O'Boyle told Nell Minow,

> so that everyone seeing [the show] could see themselves in it. We were blessed with an incredible level of talent and they have given truly exceptional performances. It was wonderful to see how their widely diverse spiritual backgrounds unified into a very moving experience—for the actors and the audience.[9]

But the production does even more to help audiences connect to its characters. While its title is an allusion to the medieval European "mystery plays"—dramatic retellings of biblical stories which, like Passion plays, began in but moved out of churches (in large part because they grew increasingly bawdy)—it also suggests this musical explores the human mysteries within the "great mystery" of Christ's death and resurrection. It asks the kind of questions one would ask of *any* story: Why did he say *that*? Why did she do *that*? How did they feel about *that*?

People ask such questions when stories truly engage them. And when stories engage people, they have an opportunity to influence, even transform, those who hear and see them.

Kevin Earley, who plays Peter in *Easter Mysteries*, said this about the piece in a video interview:

> [*Easter Mysteries* is] a nice combination of
> questions that people are going to ask, and
> questions that people are always asking
> and will continue to ask. And this [show]
> gives you a few answers—not all of them—
> and it may connect to certain people more
> profoundly than others. But it certainly
> has made me think about a lot of my life
> and what I want to be like in the future, and
> what kind of person I want to be.[10]

Ensemble member Sumayya Ali said, "The story is relatable to everybody. Anyone can empathize and relate with this. You don't have to be super-religious. But it's a human experience."[11]

And producer Ron Simons sounded a similar note: "At the end of the day they were just human beings. Even Jesus Christ was a human being. Any and everyone, I think, will be able to watch this piece, be entertained, and be inspired, and that's what gets me excited about it."[12]

Foreword

About This Viewing Guide

Easter Mysteries addresses a wide audience, Christian and non-Christian alike. This Viewing Guide, however, is designed for individuals watching the film—on their own or as part of a group—who are already familiar with Christian tradition and the Bible. At the same time, it seeks to honor the production's generous and inclusive spirit by asking Christian viewers to reconsider their own ideas and beliefs about the Easter story from other points of view.

Sessions 1–3 divide *Easter Mysteries* into three sections, each approximately a half hour long. Each session contains:

- a **summary** of the segment being viewed, so viewers can keep the whole in mind when thinking about specific details;
- a **prayer of preparation** to help Christian viewers approach this activity as more than "watching a movie," but as a spiritual discipline that can nourish their growth as followers of Jesus;
- several **reflection and discussion questions** to either provoke individual thought about and reaction to the film or use in group settings or both;
- **biblical passages** from the Common English Bible (unless otherwise noted), to facilitate quick and convenient comparison of material from *Easter Mysteries* with Scripture;

- **extended quotations** from *Easter Mysteries* lyrics, with permission from John O'Boyle, to facilitate reflection and discussion, and to serve as possible resources for personal devotion.

In addition, the Leader Helps section at the end of this guide presents suggestions for screening *Easter Mysteries* with a group in a single session.

A Final Thought

Erin Davie, who plays Mary Magdalene in *Easter Mysteries*, sums up her interpretation of the show's message this way: "Anybody can be redeemed. No matter where you come from, no matter who you are, there is hope, and there's a place for you, and there is always a possibility for a better tomorrow."[13]

May you and your congregation use this fresh and fascinating version of the Easter story as a resource for discovering new hope and new beginnings in the great mystery of Christian faith.

Preface

Creating *Easter Mysteries*

The mystical experience of God is a companion to my imagination during my creative process. The time I spend picturing a character or a scene or a song is holy for me. Even while struggling with my spiritual inadequacies writing *Easter Mysteries*, I felt this way. So, as I was drawn to the inscrutabilities surrounding Easter, it felt like guidance from God when my attention began to focus on anti-Semitism and iconography.

Long before the minister of my church, the Reverend Tricia de Beer, challenged me to write a chancel piece for our choir to perform on Palm Sunday, I had spent time researching anti-Semitism, something that has always bothered me. Over dinners with my close friend Rabbi Harold White, Jewish Chaplain of Georgetown University at the time, I was better able to understand the origins of Jewish-Christian conflict. Those conversations permeate this show.

While writing scenes, characters, and songs, the history of two thousand years of storytelling restrained me. Knowing the disciples, knowing what Jesus endures during Holy Week, and knowing that the crucifixion ends in resurrection felt too pat. Needing to reach beyond these holy figures' status as omniscient beings, I wanted to express what it might have felt like to live this story, so I imagined the disciples differently: as devout Jews following their charismatic leader. What if the disciples experienced the Last Supper with the typical optimism of a Seder, not worrying about Judas's kiss? This was how I imagined all of *Easter Mysteries*: going inside the flat iconic character or scene to participate in it.

The scenes of the Passion are relatively standard, beginning with the entrance into Jerusalem and ending at or just after the crucifixion. Developing ideas for staging the resurrection was more complicated as resurrection literature appears infrequently. Once we leave the empty tomb, time and place become amorphous, especially among the Gospels. Is it one woman or three who go to the tomb? And if it's three, which three? How does one depict Jesus after the crucifixion? Can you touch him? Can you hold him tightly? There are widely divergent views on this as reflected in the multitude of Christian sects. *Easter Mysteries* is my exploration into this territory, an attempt to respond to these questions.

Easter Mysteries started as a chancel piece performed by our church choir and then took on a life of its own with the choir traveling to other cities in Maryland before going to Wales and England. I developed two additional productions in New York City, burnished by Broadway talent.

Preface

The first production was staged; the second was done as an oratorio. Finally, under the encouragement of Fathom Events, a third performance was generated to make the film.

When the director, Daniel Goldstein, and I set out to cast this film, we had no preconceived ideas other than we wanted the cast to look like America. The talent that responded was like manna from heaven. The mystical experience of God has accompanied me throughout the amazing journey that *Easter Mysteries* has been in my life, and "dreams that I had never dreamed, they also have come true, now comes the dawn."

John O'Boyle
October 1, 2019

Session 1
Passion

Summary (Scenes 1–8)

Jesus's excited followers march to Jerusalem, where they expect to see their rabbi perform even greater wonders than he already has. Only Peter's jealousy of Jesus's attention to Mary Magdalene injects a sour note into the celebratory atmosphere.

Days later, Jesus and his disciples gather in an upper room to celebrate the Passover seder. Most of the disciples recall with glee Jesus's dramatic protest against the Temple moneychangers earlier in the week, but Judas worries that Jesus upset powerful people, who now say they want to talk with him.

During the meal, Jesus predicts a friend will betray him. After Judas leaves to keep an appointment, Jesus encourages his disciples to remember him with the Passover bread and wine once he is no longer with them.

Mary Magdalene meets Jesus and the disciples after the seder, in the garden of Gethsemane. Jesus tenderly asks her to leave before he and the others face a hard testing. He asks the others to stay and pray with him. Peter declares unending loyalty to Jesus, but Jesus says Peter will deny him three times before morning. As Jesus prays God would spare him but still submits to God's will, Judas arrives with an armed crowd. Jesus urges his followers not to defend him as he is arrested.

Outside the house of Caiaphas, the high priest, Peter encounters a servant who is Naomi, the woman to whom he was betrothed but whom he left so he could follow Jesus. Naomi urges Peter to either come back to Galilee with her, or to go and defend the man he chose to follow, because Jesus has been condemned to death. She tries to tell others Peter is one of Jesus's followers, but Peter denies the fact three times before a cock crows at sunrise. Hearing the cock crow, Peter runs away, leaving Naomi alone again.

In rapid succession, Caiaphas, Pilate, and Herod all stand in judgment of Jesus. None of these authorities wants final responsibility for deciding Jesus's fate, yet all are certain of his guilt and their blamelessness.

Meanwhile, Peter and Judas meet. Judas says he believed the authorities only wanted to talk with Jesus; now, he is on his way to return the money he received for leading them to Jesus. For his part, Peter is wracked with guilt about denying Jesus, and is on his way to hang himself. Judas urges him not to and wrestles his rope noose from him, assuring him Jesus will forgive them both. Peter tells Judas that Jesus has been condemned. Judas runs to Caiaphas's house, convinced he can return the money and that Jesus will be freed.

Crucified on Golgotha, Jesus prays to God, asking why God has abandoned him. He prays for his followers, then commits his spirit to God. Pilate, in mocking "respect" for the Sabbath, orders a centurion to end the execution. The centurion reports breaking the other criminals' legs to hurry their deaths, and piercing Jesus's side to confirm Jesus was already dead.

After the crucifixion, the centurion and Peter meet. With keen interest, the centurion asks Peter what will happen to Jesus's movement now that Jesus is dead. He tells Peter that seeing Jesus die moved him to declare Jesus "God's own son." Peter and Jesus's other followers sing their commitment to remembering Jesus and his dreams for the world.

Prayer of Preparation

Holy God, in Jesus's death and resurrection you reveal the mystery of your love for us and for the world. Through this presentation of Christ's Passion in a new way, may your Spirit grant new insights into all you have given us in our Savior, and new resolve and resources to respond as his faithful followers.

Watch *Easter Mysteries*

Watch *Easter Mysteries*, scenes 1–8 (0:00:00–0:35:25).

Questions for Reflection

Scene 1—Entry into Jerusalem

1. *Easter Mysteries* opens with a depiction of Jesus's entrance into Jerusalem but focuses on the crowd following him rather than on Jesus himself. How does this choice change your perspective on the events of Palm Sunday?
2. The crowd anticipates wonders and miracles. Have you ever hoped for miracles, as the crowd does? Were your hopes fulfilled or were you disappointed? How did you respond?
3. What does the dialogue between Peter and Judas tell us about these two disciples and their relationships to Jesus? Why do you think Jesus's disciples couldn't understand what he meant by "going to Jerusalem to die"?

Scene 2—Last Supper

4. Why Judas betrayed Jesus is one of history's most frequently debated questions. What does this scene suggest about him and his motives? How do you respond to this interpretation?
5. The disciples recall Jesus's cleansing of the Temple **(Matthew 21:12-13; Mark 11:15-18; Luke 19:45-48; John 2:13-22)**. What do Jesus's actions tell us about him? What do the disciples' reactions tell us about them?

6. The refrain of Peter's hymn for Passover asks, "What do we learn from looking at our past?" How does this song connect the disciples' present to Israel's past? What conclusions do the disciples draw from those connections?
7. What formal or informal rituals does your congregation use to look to and learn from its past? How do you practice this looking and learning in your own life? When have you drawn reliable conclusions from it, when have you not—and how do you tell the difference?
8. What meaning does Jesus give to the bread and the wine in this scene? How are these meanings like or unlike the ways you think about the bread and the cup when you observe Holy Communion (the Lord's Supper; the Eucharist)?

This is my body.
This is my blood.
Celebrate your memory of me!

You are my body.
You are my blood.
Be the child of God that you can be!
Follow me and I'll set your spirit free.

My hands no longer till the soil.
My arms won't reach the vine.
So you must be my bread of life,
Your love must flow like wine.

This Is My Body

This is my body.
This is my blood.
Celebrate your memory of me!

You are my body.
You are my blood.
Be the child of God that you can be!
Follow me and I'll set your spirit free.

My hands no longer till the soil.
My arms won't reach the vine.
So you must be my bread of life,
Your love must flow like wine.

You are my body.
You are my blood.
Be the child of God that you can be!
Celebrate this in memory of me.

Passion

You are my body.
You are my blood.
Be the child of God that you can be!
Celebrate this in memory of me.[1]

9. Read these passages from **1 Corinthians**:

> Isn't the cup of blessing that we bless a sharing in the blood of Christ? Isn't the loaf of bread that we break a sharing in the body of Christ? Since there is one loaf of bread, we who are many are one body, because we all share the one loaf of bread. **(10:16-17)**
>
> First of all, when you meet together as a church, I hear that there are divisions among you, and I partly believe it. It's necessary that there are groups among you, to make it clear who is genuine. So when you get together in one place, it isn't to eat the Lord's meal. Each of you goes ahead and eats a private meal. One person goes hungry while another is drunk. Don't you have houses to eat and drink in? Or do you look down on God's churches and humiliate those who have nothing? What can I say to you? Will I praise you? No, I don't praise you in this.
>
> I received a tradition from the Lord, which I also handed on to you: on the night on which he was betrayed, the Lord Jesus took bread. After giving thanks, he broke it and said, "This is my body, which is for you; do this to remember me." He did the same

thing with the cup, after they had eaten, saying, "This cup is the new covenant in my blood. Every time you drink it, do this to remember me." Every time you eat this bread and drink this cup, you broadcast the death of the Lord until he comes.

This is why those who eat the bread or drink the cup of the Lord inappropriately will be guilty of the Lord's body and blood. Each individual should test himself or herself and eat from the bread and drink from the cup in that way. Those who eat and drink without correctly understanding the body are eating and drinking their own judgment. **(11:18-29)**

Henry Rietz, a religious studies professor at Grinnell College, writes:

> In *Easter Mysteries*, O'Boyle is effectively reinterpreting the elements of the Eucharist to promote a community that remembers and embodies the spirit of Jesus. Here the notion of Jesus's followers remembering Jesus and embodying Jesus—being the body of Christ—is a kind of incarnational theology, not of God becoming flesh in Jesus, but Jesus becoming flesh in his followers.[2]

How is this interpretation like and unlike Paul's emphasis on community when discussing the Lord's Supper? How does your congregation celebrate the Lord's Supper (Holy Communion; Eucharist) in ways that encourage participants to experience themselves and one another as "one body" in Christ? What words and actions could further emphasize this aspect of the sacrament?

Scene 3—Gethsemane

10. In the Gospels, Mary Magdalene is not present at Gethsemane as she briefly is in *Easter Mysteries*. What do we learn about her as a character in this scene? Why does Peter treat her as he does?
11. Compare and contrast Jesus's prayer in Gethsemane in this scene with the Gospel accounts of it (**Matthew 26:36-46; Mark 14:32-42; Luke 22:39-46**). What does the play emphasize about Jesus's prayer, and why? What significance, if any, do you see in Jesus finishing his prayer after Judas's kiss and his arrest?

> *Take this cup of sorrow,*
> *Let it pass from me!*
> *I am sad unto death*
> *For what I'd hoped to be.*
>
> *Father, where's your vision?*
> *Was it just a dream?*
> *Have we searched every path*
> *As hopeless as they seem?*
>
> *Anything is possible,*
> *My work has just begun,*
> *But if it is not possible*
> *Then let your will be done!*

See your children broken?
Hear their misery!
Lonely, lost, suffering,
Oh, suffer them to me!
And if I then must drain this cup,
Then pass the cup to me![3]

Scene 4—Peter's Denial

12. Although Scripture mentions Jesus healing Simon Peter's mother-in-law (**Matthew 8:14-17; Mark 1:29-31; Luke 4:38-39**), *Easter Mysteries* invents the character of Naomi. How closely can you relate to her? How sympathetic do you find her? What does she add to the Easter story as this play tells it?
13. Naomi alludes to the fact that her former betrothed has two names: "I'm done waiting now, Simon. You choose. Go ahead and be Peter or whoever you are around him." Read about how and why Jesus gave Simon a new name in **Matthew 16:13-20**. How does this Scripture affect the way you watch Naomi and Simon Peter's interaction in this scene?
14. When have you been torn between two identities, as Peter is in this scene? When have you "run away," literally or figuratively, from those you care about and who care about you? What, if anything, would you do differently if you could relive that situation?
15. Have you ever been torn between your loyalties and responsibilities to other people and

Gethsemane

Take this cup of sorrow,
Let it pass from me!
I am sad unto death
For what I'd hoped to be.

Father, where's your vision?
Was it just a dream?
Have we searched every path
As hopeless as they seem?

Anything is possible,
My work has just begun,
But if it is not possible
Then let your will be done!

See your children broken?
Hear their misery!
Lonely, lost, suffering,
Oh, suffer them to me!
And if I then must drain this cup,
Then pass the cup to me!

your faith? What choice did you make? What happened because of your choice?

Scene 5—Judgment Before Caiaphas, Pilate, and Herod

16. *Easter Mysteries* presents Jesus's death sentence as the end result of competing interests and complicated conflicts. What does the song say about how and why each of the men listed below regarded Jesus as a problem or threat?

    - **Caiaphas**, the Jewish high priest
    - **Pilate**, the Roman, non-Jewish governor of Roman-occupied Judea
    - **Herod**, the ruler of Galilee appointed by and friendly with the Roman Empire

    How, if at all, does this play's view of who bears blame for Jesus's death differ from other views with which you may be familiar?

17. In **Matthew 27:24**, Pilate washes his hands to symbolically declare his innocence in Jesus's death. In this scene, all three leaders "wash their hands" of Jesus. Have you ever felt like "washing your hands" of Jesus? Why? Have you ever done so? What happened?

18. Unlike many traditional Passion plays, *Easter Mysteries* omits any direct reference to **Matthew 27:25**, a verse Christians have abused for centuries to hold all Jews everywhere and in all times guilty for Jesus's death. But this

song does allude to the crowd's role: "The people will decide your fate," "So off you go to see your peers / They'll do what they will do."[4] How can Christians today discuss the Gospel accounts of the people's role without perpetrating anti-Semitic, anti-Jewish hatred?

19. Where have you witnessed, heard about, or personally experienced injustices and abuses of power in today's world? What wisdom or warnings does the story of Jesus's trial give us for facing and responding to such situations?

Scene 6—Two Paths

20. In the *Easter Mysteries* script, this scene is titled "Two Paths." Why do you think the playwright created this scene and gave it that title?
21. Judas tells Peter it's not our mistakes that matter, but what we do with them. Knowing what **Matthew 27:3-5** says Judas did about his mistake, how do you react to Judas's statement in this scene?
22. Judas says he expects Jesus will be angry with him and Peter but will forgive them "like always." Do you think Judas could have been, or even was, forgiven? Why or why not?

Scene 7—Golgotha

23. As each Gospel does, *Easter Mysteries* includes some details about Jesus's crucifixion

while omitting others. How do the details it includes, individually and together, help the audience find meaning in Jesus's death?

24. Jesus's song draws on two of the traditional "seven last words" Jesus spoke from his cross:

    - "My God, my God, why have you left me?" (**Matthew 27:46; Mark 15:34**; compare **Psalm 22**)
    - "Father, *into your hands I entrust my life.*" (**Luke 23:46**; compare **Psalm 31**)

    These words from the cross capture two extremes of human experience: utter abandonment and complete trust. When have you been able to identify with either or both of Jesus's words? How have those experiences shaped your faith? How have they shaped your relationships with other people?

25. Who is the woman singing above and with Jesus as he dies? What does she represent? How does her presence help communicate the meaning of Jesus's death in *Easter Mysteries*?

26. In *Easter Mysteries*, Jesus prays for his disciples from his cross. Compare his prayer to the prayer recorded in **John 17**:

    > [Jesus said,] "I'm praying for them. I'm not praying for the world but for those you gave me, because they are yours. Everything that is mine is yours and everything that is yours is mine; I have been glorified in them.

Passion

I'm no longer in the world, but they are in the world, even as I'm coming to you. Holy Father, watch over them in your name, the name you gave me, that they will be one just as we are one. When I was with them, I watched over them in your name, the name you gave to me, and I kept them safe. None of them were lost, except the one who was destined for destruction, so that scripture would be fulfilled. Now I'm coming to you and I say these things while I'm in the world so that they can share completely in my joy. I gave your word to them and the world hated them, because they don't belong to this world, just as I don't belong to this world. I'm not asking that you take them out of this world but that you keep them safe from the evil one. They don't belong to this world, just as I don't belong to this world. Make them holy in the truth; your word is truth. As you sent me into the world, so I have sent them into the world. I made myself holy on their behalf so that they also would be made holy in the truth.

"I'm not praying only for them but also for those who believe in me because of their word. I pray they will be one, Father, just as you are in me and I am in you. I pray that they also will be in us, so that the world will believe that you sent me. I've given them the glory that you gave me so that they can be one just as we are one. I'm in them and you are in me so that they will be made perfectly one. Then the world will know that you sent me and that you have loved them just as you loved me." **(vv. 9-23)**

What does Jesus want for those who follow him? When, inside *or* outside the church, have you experienced the kind of community Jesus envisions for his followers? How, if ever, have you experienced power knowing someone else was praying on your behalf?

Scene 8—Requiem

27. How does the play's conversation between Peter and the centurion foreshadow what Jesus's followers will do when Jesus is gone?
28. As Jesus leaves the stage during the song, he moves through the ensemble and pauses next to Judas. What do you think this staging decision signifies?
29. How do Peter and the disciples' memories of Jesus affect them in this scene's song? How have your memories of people important to you who have died shaped (and how do they continue to shape) the ways you go on living?

> *Your hope won't die here.*
> *I will remember how*
> *To sing at sunrise*
> *And plan the day.*
>
> *Your words aren't silent.*
> *I won't abandon them.*

Passion

You've learned my sorrows,
And so, I pray.

Your memory now flows
Through my heart and sets my spirit free.
It matters not what greater be,
I give myself to you, and you give all to me.

Now in this moment,
We will remember you,
And what you promised
And what you hoped
And what you dreamed.
We are your body, we are your blood,
Your song![5]

♪

Session 2

Resurrection

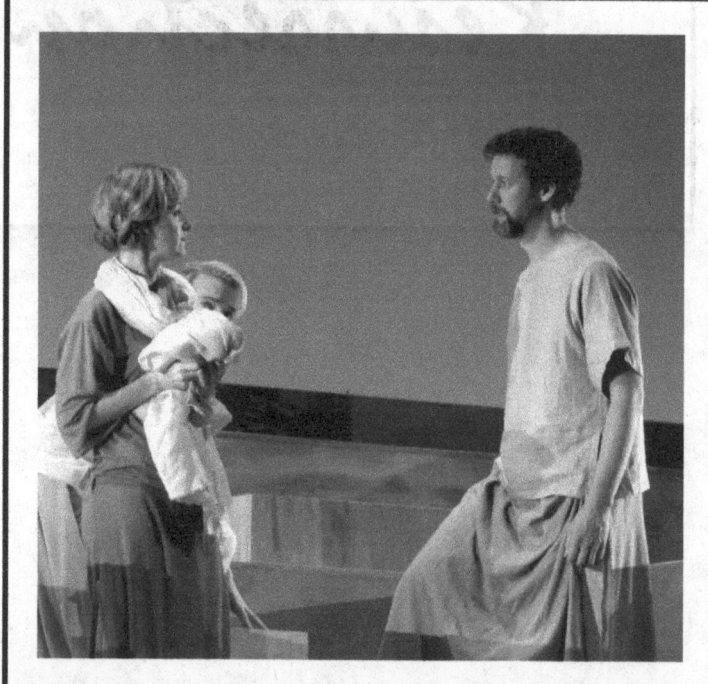

Summary (Scenes 9–12)

Mary Magdalene, Miriam, and Joanna go to Jesus's tomb early on Sunday morning. They find the tomb empty and unguarded. Suddenly, they experience a vision in which heaven proclaims good news: Jesus has been raised from death.

Frightened, they run to the upper room where Jesus's male disciples are hiding from Jesus's enemies even as they confront their own guilt for having abandoned him and their fears and doubts about their future without him. The women tell the men what they have experienced, only to find each saw and heard the same message in different ways.

Peter angrily rejects the women's report, but John suggests they go to Jesus's tomb to see for themselves. After John and Peter see the empty tomb for themselves, they leave, but Mary remains behind. She encounters the risen Jesus, although she does not recognize him until he calls her by name. Jesus tells Mary he will soon be ascending to God, but will also always be with Mary and his other followers, working through them to replace sorrow with hope.

Prayer of Preparation

Living God, death itself could not hold your servant Jesus in its grip. As we watch and reflect on the story of his resurrection, may your Spirit surprise us again with the glad news of your victory. May we go and tell others, not only in word but also in deed, that the One we all seek is alive and active, wiping away tears and loving us always.

Watch *Easter Mysteries*

Watch *Easter Mysteries*, Scenes 9–12 (0:35:37–1:00:54).

Scene 9—On the Path to the Tomb

1. How is the women's approach to Jesus's tomb in Scene 9 like and unlike the various Gospel accounts?
2. Why do you think each of the women in Scene 9 expresses different thoughts and feelings about their shared trip to the tomb? Do you find you relate to any one of the women more than the others? Why or why not?
3. Why is Mary Magdalene committed to getting to the tomb in Scene 9? When have you been committed to a "quest" other people had doubts about? What did you do, and what were the results?
4. In the scene, Mary enters Jesus's tomb first, telling Miriam and Joanna, "Follow me." Why

might the playwright have decided for Mary to echo Jesus's frequent words to his disciples at this moment?

5. How would you explain Joanna's sudden surge of hope near the end of the scene? Have you ever had an experience like hers, of "dancing tears and fears away"? What happened?

6. How might the women's individual and shared experience of the path be a helpful metaphor for life together in communities of faith today?

Scene 10—At the Tomb

7. The Latin phrase *Quem Quaeritis*—"Whom do you seek?"—comes from a tenth-century chant that inspired a liturgical dialogue in which male celebrants essentially "acted out" the women's visit to Jesus's tomb. Some historians trace a line from this ritual to not only the "mystery plays" of the Middle Ages but also the sixteenth-century dramas of Shakespeare and his contemporaries. In fact, according to some, this brief ritual gave drama as a whole a future in Western civilization.[1]

8. While *Quem Quaeritis* isn't a verbatim quote from the Latin Bible, it closely paraphrases Luke's story of Easter morning:

> Very early in the morning on the first day
> of the week, the women went to the tomb,
> bringing the fragrant spices they had
> prepared. They found the stone rolled away

from the tomb, but when they went in, they didn't find the body of the Lord Jesus. They didn't know what to make of this. Suddenly, two men were standing beside them in gleaming bright clothing. The women were frightened and bowed their faces toward the ground, but the men said to them, "Why do you look for the living among the dead? He isn't here, but has been raised. Remember what he told you while he was still in Galilee, that the Human One must be handed over to sinners, be crucified, and on the third day rise again." Then they remembered his words. When they returned from the tomb, they reported all these things to the eleven and all the others. It was Mary Magdalene, Joanna, Mary the mother of James, and the other women with them who told these things to the apostles. **(Luke 24:1-10)**

How do you react to the dramatization in *Easter Mysteries* of the women's discovery at Jesus's tomb?

9. Like the New Testament, *Easter Mysteries* does not depict Jesus's resurrection itself (though **Matthew 28:2** comes closest). Why do you think none of the Gospels directly describes this most important miracle? What do dramas gain or lose by following the Gospels' lead?

10. The question the angels ask in Luke is not about *whom* the women seek but *where* they seek him (a question *Easter Mysteries* directly addresses in a later scene). When, if ever, have

Resurrection

you sought Jesus in the wrong places or people? How did you discover your mistake, and what did you do to make it right?

11. The scene ends with the women running from the tomb in fear. In this respect the scene follows Mark's account of the first Easter morning:

> When the Sabbath was over, Mary Magdalene, Mary the mother of James, and Salome bought spices so that they could go and anoint Jesus' dead body. Very early on the first day of the week, just after sunrise, they came to the tomb. They were saying to each other, "Who's going to roll the stone away from the entrance for us?" When they looked up, they saw that the stone had been rolled away. (And it was a very large stone!) Going into the tomb, they saw a young man in a white robe seated on the right side; and they were startled. But he said to them, "Don't be alarmed! You are looking for Jesus of Nazareth, who was crucified. He has been raised. He isn't here. Look, here's the place where they laid him. Go, tell his disciples, especially Peter, that he is going ahead of you into Galilee. You will see him there, just as he told you." Overcome with terror and dread, they fled from the tomb. They said nothing to anyone, because they were afraid. **(Mark 16:1-8)**

12. Why, despite angelic reassurances, are the women frightened by their discovery? Why

should the announcement that, as *Easter Mysteries* puts it, "death is different than before" be cause for alarm instead of—or as well as—dazing, amazing "good news"?

Scene 11—The Upper Room

13. How do the disciples' dialogue and song in this scene serve to make them relatable characters? With which of the disciples do you identify most closely at this point, and why?
14. The women's differing accounts of what they saw and heard at Jesus's tomb reflect some of the differences in the Gospels' accounts. Compare **Luke 24:1-10** and **Mark 16:1-8** (printed above, in Scene 10) with **Matthew 28:1-10**:

> After the Sabbath, at dawn on the first day of the week, Mary Magdalene and the other Mary came to look at the tomb. Look, there was a great earthquake, for an angel from the Lord came down from heaven. Coming to the stone, he rolled it away and sat on it. Now his face was like lightning and his clothes as white as snow. The guards were so terrified of him that they shook with fear and became like dead men. But the angel said to the women, "Don't be afraid. I know that you are looking for Jesus who was crucified. He isn't here, because he's been raised from the dead, just as he said. Come, see the place where they laid him. Now hurry, go and tell his disciples, 'He's been

raised from the dead. He's going on ahead of you to Galilee. You will see him there.' I've given the message to you."

With great fear and excitement, they hurried away from the tomb and ran to tell his disciples. But Jesus met them and greeted them. They came and grabbed his feet and worshipped him. Then Jesus said to them, "Don't be afraid. Go and tell my brothers that I am going into Galilee. They will see me there."

Why does Peter doubt the women? Have you, like him and other male disciples in this scene, ever wondered or worried whether the news of the Resurrection is "nonsense" (Luke 24:11)? How did (or how do) you deal with such doubts? What would you say to someone else who is feeling doubt and skepticism about the Resurrection?

15. Henry Rietz writes:

> One of the things that I really appreciate about O'Boyle's work is that he represents ... how Jesus' followers struggled to make meaning of Jesus' teachings, death and resurrection. A great example of this is the testimonies of Mary, Joanna, and Miriam struggling to make sense of the announcement "Quem Quaeritis" and even disagreeing over what they heard or saw ... pointing us to the truth [that] is not in consistency or "clarity" or historicity.[2]

What do you think about the differences among the New Testament stories of the first Easter? How important or unimportant are they to you as you "make meaning" of the news of the Resurrection? How do you respond to Professor Rietz's statement that the truth of the Resurrection is not "in consistency or 'clarity' or historicity"?

Scene 12—At the Tomb

16. This scene closely, but not slavishly, follows the Gospel of John's account of the first Easter:

    > Early in the morning of the first day of the week, while it was still dark, Mary Magdalene came to the tomb and saw that the stone had been taken away from the tomb. She ran to Simon Peter and the other disciple, the one whom Jesus loved, and said, "They have taken the Lord from the tomb, and we don't know where they've put him." Peter and the other disciple left to go to the tomb. They were running together, but the other disciple ran faster than Peter and was the first to arrive at the tomb. Bending down to take a look, he saw the linen cloths lying there, but he didn't go in. Following him, Simon Peter entered the tomb and saw the linen cloths lying there. He also saw the face cloth that had been on Jesus' head. It wasn't with the other clothes

but was folded up in its own place. Then the other disciple, the one who arrived at the tomb first, also went inside. He saw and believed. They didn't yet understand the scripture that Jesus must rise from the dead. Then the disciples returned to the place where they were staying.

Mary stood outside near the tomb, crying. As she cried, she bent down to look into the tomb. She saw two angels dressed in white, seated where the body of Jesus had been, one at the head and one at the foot. The angels asked her, "Woman, why are you crying?"

She replied, "They have taken away my Lord, and I don't know where they've put him." As soon as she had said this, she turned around and saw Jesus standing there, but she didn't know it was Jesus.

Jesus said to her, "Woman, why are you crying? Who are you looking for?"

Thinking he was the gardener, she replied, "Sir, if you have carried him away, tell me where you have put him and I will get him."

Jesus said to her, "Mary."

She turned and said to him in Aramaic, "Rabbouni" (which means "Teacher").

Jesus said to her, "Don't hold on to me, for I haven't yet gone up to my Father. Go to my brothers and sisters and tell them, 'I'm going up to my Father and your Father, to my God and your God.'"

I Will Wipe Away Each Tear

Heaven knows you've changed me, I don't have a clue,
How could you slip by my guard?
I would not allow love, suddenly there's you,
Walking through a door I thought I'd barred.
All at once my life has life, more complete and full of joy,
Unexpected dreams come true.
And I'll always cherish the part of me that's you.

I could hardly leave you now, I'm a part of you.
You are in my every thought, everything I do . . .

Resurrection

> Mary Magdalene left and announced to the disciples, "I've seen the Lord." Then she told them what he said to her. (**John 20:1-18**)

What dramatic licenses does *Easter Mysteries* take with this passage, and why do you think it takes them? How do you respond to the changes? How, if at all, does what it keeps the same influence how you read the Scripture?

17. Mary wonders why Peter can't see the change Jesus caused in her life and asks John whether he sees her any differently than he used to. Of Mary's prior life, Scripture says only that Jesus cast out seven demons from her (**Luke 8:2; Mark 16:9**). In some nonbiblical traditions as well as in some modern interpretations, Mary is cast as a former prostitute. What do you glean about *Easter Mysteries*' Mary as she was before she knew Jesus?

18. John tells Mary, "Jesus saw things in all of us differently." When and how has your faith led you to see good and holy things in people that others don't—and that they perhaps don't even see in themselves? How does and how can Jesus's church encourage this kind of Christlike vision in our world today?

19. Unlike the Gospel accounts but like the ancient *Quem Quaeritis* liturgical drama, *Easter Mysteries* places some importance on Jesus's burial shroud. John says, "It may help the others if they have something to see." What

role do visible and tangible objects play in your faith? How can things to see, touch, and hold be aids to belief? How can they become hindrances?
20. Peter asks Mary, "Why would angels appear to you and not to me?" What do you think motivates his question? How is Peter's question relevant to issues of who has authority to speak for God today?
21. How would you describe *Easter Mysteries*' depiction of Mary and Jesus's relationship? What creates and sustains the connection they share? How is their relationship like and unlike the relationship any believer can have with Jesus?
22. What links do Jesus and Mary's duet make to Revelation's vision of the future, and how does it connect that vision to what Jesus calls his followers to do in the present?

> I heard a loud voice from the throne say, "Look! God's dwelling is here with humankind. He will dwell with them, and they will be his peoples. God himself will be with them as their God. He will wipe away every tear from their eyes. Death will be no more. There will be no mourning, crying, or pain anymore, for the former things have passed away." **(Revelation 21:3-4)**

23. In Jesus's and Mary's duet, they sing to each other, "You will live forever, the part of me that's you." How is this concept of living

forever like or unlike what you think of as eternal life?
24. In the song, Mary describes how she has changed because of Jesus. How can you relate to her experience of Jesus's presence in her life? What are some specific changes you attribute to your relationship with Jesus? What would you say is "the part of you that's him?"
25. Jesus tells Mary, "I cannot do the things I need to do unless you help me." What do you think about this statement as a description of the church's purpose?

> *Heaven knows you've changed me, I don't*
>   *have a clue,*
> *How could you slip by my guard?*
> *I would not allow love, suddenly there's you,*
> *Walking through a door I thought I'd barred.*
> *All at once my life has life, more complete*
>   *and full of joy,*
> *Unexpected dreams come true.*
> *And I'll always cherish the part of me that's you.*
>
> *I could hardly leave you now, I'm a part of you.*
> *You are in my every thought, everything I do.*
> *You have changed the way I hear, changed*
>   *the way I see,*
> *You have changed the way I feel, such a*
>   *different me!*
>
> *Never think you leave me, such a foolish*
>   *thought,*

Linger, let me touch your heart.
Let me reassure you, this is what you taught,
You stay with me even when we part.
When I'm merely dust again, when my
  name is long forgot,
Even when the world is through,
You will live forever, the part of me that's you.[3]

Session 3
Mission

Summary (Scene 13)

Mary Magdalene returns to the upper room, telling Jesus's followers she has seen him. While some disciples are convinced, Thomas and Peter remain skeptical. Two disciples, Cleopas and Simon, return from their trip to Emmaus with a story corroborating Mary's: they met the risen Jesus on the road, though they did not recognize him until he broke bread with them.

Peter sends Thomas to investigate this "conspiracy" about Jesus's supposed return from death but confesses that he is afraid. He fears that he hasn't seen the risen Jesus because Jesus has not forgiven him for his denials. As Mary tries to persuade Peter that Jesus still loves him, many other followers arrive with their own stories of seeing him alive. Convinced Jesus must be alive but even more upset that he has not seen him, Peter wonders whether he deserves to be the leader of the group.

Suddenly, Peter hears but does not see Jesus. Only after Jesus convinces Peter to forgive himself is Peter able to see him, to accept Jesus's forgiveness, and to hear his command to show heaven to the world.

Thomas returns, having found no evidence that Jesus is alive. He is upset to learn Peter now believes the story, but quickly believes it himself when he sees Jesus, who offers to put Thomas's hand in his own pierced side.

Jesus leaves his disciples and ascends to God, but not before promising he will be with them when they care for others. Although his followers are initially confused and upset after Jesus leaves, their prayer for the Holy Spirit's arrival leads to their renewed confidence and a new sense of possibility and purpose as they face the world.

Prayer of Preparation

Living God, you send your Spirit to kindle new hope and new dreams within us, and to empower us to do your work in this world until it becomes the new heaven and earth you have promised. Help us to find our place in the ongoing story of Easter, sensing and serving our risen Savior in the ways he has taught us, following him until your dawn fully breaks over all things. Amen.

Watch *Easter Mysteries*

Watch *Easter Mysteries*, Scene 13 (1:00:55–1:28:46).

"On the Road to Emmaus"

1. Cleopas and Simon's song about their encounter with the risen Jesus is based on **Luke 24:13-35**:

Mission

On that same day, two disciples were traveling to a village called Emmaus, about seven miles from Jerusalem. They were talking to each other about everything that had happened. While they were discussing these things, Jesus himself arrived and joined them on their journey. They were prevented from recognizing him.

He said to them, "What are you talking about as you walk along?" They stopped, their faces downcast.

The one named Cleopas replied, "Are you the only visitor to Jerusalem who is unaware of the things that have taken place there over the last few days?"

He said to them, "What things?"

They said to him, "The things about Jesus of Nazareth. Because of his powerful deeds and words, he was recognized by God and all the people as a prophet. But our chief priests and our leaders handed him over to be sentenced to death, and they crucified him. We had hoped he was the one who would redeem Israel. All these things happened three days ago. But there's more: Some women from our group have left us stunned. They went to the tomb early this morning and didn't find his body. They came to us saying that they had even seen a vision of angels who told them he is alive. Some of those who were with us went to the tomb and found things just as the women said. They didn't see him."

Then Jesus said to them, "You foolish people! Your dull minds keep you from believing all that the prophets talked about. Wasn't it necessary for the Christ to suffer these things and then enter into his glory?" Then he interpreted for them the things written about himself in all the scriptures, starting with Moses and going through all the Prophets.

When they came to Emmaus, he acted as if he was going on ahead. But they urged him, saying, "Stay with us. It's nearly evening, and the day is almost over." So he went in to stay with them. After he took his seat at the table with them, he took the bread, blessed and broke it, and gave it to them. Their eyes were opened and they recognized him, but he disappeared from their sight. They said to each other, "Weren't our hearts on fire when he spoke to us along the road and when he explained the scriptures for us?"

They got up right then and returned to Jerusalem. They found the eleven and their companions gathered together. They were saying to each other, "The Lord really has risen! He appeared to Simon!" Then the two disciples described what had happened along the road and how Jesus was made known to them as he broke the bread.

What do you think prevented these disciples from immediately recognizing Jesus? Why do you think Jesus disappears from these

On the Road to Emmaus

On the road to Emmaus,
Life is never quite what it seems.
What starts out a simple journey
Quickly travels past your dreams.

disciples as soon as they recognize him? What does this story suggest about the importance of offering hospitality as a part of following Jesus?
2. Jesus's interpretation of the Scriptures helps prepare these disciples to recognize Jesus. When, if ever, have you felt your "heart on fire" as you studied Scripture? How important is regular reading and study of Scripture to you as you follow Jesus, and why?
3. The disciples finally recognize Jesus as he breaks bread with them. His actions mirror those he took at the Last Supper (Luke 22:19), and the actions taken in his name in celebrations of Holy Communion. How often, if ever, do you find Communion to be a powerful meeting with Jesus?
4. In *Easter Mysteries*, Cleopas and Simon sing:

> *On the road to Emmaus,*
> *Life is never quite what it seems.*
> *What starts out a simple journey*
> *Quickly travels past your dreams.*[1]

J. D. Webster, the actor who plays Simon, calls this song "a metaphor for life. We meet a stranger, not knowing that it's actually Christ. I think that speaks a lot about how our lives sometimes flow. We don't see the good right in front of our eyes."[2] Have you ever had such an experience? At what point did you suddenly see the good that had been before you all

Mission

along or realize that what you thought was a "simple journey" had in fact brought you "past your dreams"?

"Now Comes the Dawn"

5. Much Christian tradition calls Mary Magdalene "the apostle to the apostles." How is this title for Mary like or unlike how you have seen her remembered in the church and in popular culture? How does *Easter Mysteries* show Mary living into the meaning of this title?
6. Before Jesus appears in the upper room, Peter says, "I don't understand why I find myself so unsettled by Mary and her joy. It makes me angry. And if she has seen him and now others, what does that say about me?" If you were a character in the play, what would you say to Peter in response?
7. Peter asks Mary, "What if [Jesus's] grace isn't for everyone?" Have you ever wondered, as Peter does, whether some things are "so terrible" Jesus can't or won't forgive them? What things, and why?
8. In her song, Mary asks Peter, "What if, when you search the loneliness that you may feel / You found nothing but great love surrounding you?" When have your feelings of loneliness and fear kept you from experiencing God's love for you? What about other people's love for you? How, if ever, has your community of faith helped you move through those feelings,

as Mary and the disciples are trying to help Peter in this scene?

"Good News" (reprise)

9. The followers who stream into the upper room singing of Jesus's resurrection mention appearances that have no direct counterpart in the Gospels—Jesus at the crossroads, by the river, in the meadow—but that evoke such verses as **John 20:20**; **Acts 13:30**; and **1 Corinthians 15:5-6**. Do such "untold stories" of the risen Christ's appearances add to or detract from the credibility of the Resurrection claim for you? Why? What might we infer about the Resurrection from the fact that not all of Jesus's followers experienced his risen presence in exactly the same way, at exactly the same time?

10. Have you ever felt as Peter does in this scene before Jesus appears to him: wanting to believe as others believe, but unable to do so? How did you (or how do you still) deal with such times? How does your community of faith support those who struggle to believe?

"Feed My Sheep"

11. Compare and contrast Peter's meeting with the risen Jesus in *Easter Mysteries* with their conversation in **John 21:15-19**:

When they finished eating, Jesus asked Simon Peter, "Simon son of John, do you love me more than these?"

Simon replied, "Yes, Lord, you know I love you."

Jesus said to him, "Feed my lambs." Jesus asked a second time, "Simon son of John, do you love me?"

Simon replied, "Yes, Lord, you know I love you."

Jesus said to him, "Take care of my sheep." He asked a third time, "Simon son of John, do you love me?"

Peter was sad that Jesus asked him a third time, "Do you love me?" He replied, "Lord, you know everything; you know I love you."

Jesus said to him, "Feed my sheep. I assure you that when you were younger you tied your own belt and walked around wherever you wanted. When you grow old, you will stretch out your hands and another will tie your belt and lead you where you don't want to go." He said this to show the kind of death by which Peter would glorify God. After saying this, Jesus said to Peter, "Follow me."

Why does Jesus ask Peter about his love three times? What do you think Jesus means by telling Peter, "Feed my sheep?" Why does Jesus choose this moment to talk about Peter's future death?

12. The song in *Easter Mysteries* focuses not on Peter's death but on the life Jesus calls him to live:

    How can you show heaven
    To a world that's so blind
    If there are shackles on your mind?

    How does our inability to see the risen Jesus in our communities and in our own lives keep us from showing him to the world? What can we do to discern him more clearly in order to fulfill the mission he gives his church?

13. In the song, Jesus suggests Peter will not be able to see him unless he forgives himself:

    Start with your own healing,
    Stop your spirit's reeling,
    Does this seem a good plan to you?

    When was a time you struggled to forgive yourself? Were you able to do so? If so, how? If not, why not? To what extent do we need to forgive ourselves in order to believe and experience God's forgiveness?

14. *Easter Mysteries* director Daniel Goldstein says, "The story is about forgiveness, and what all religion really should do, but mostly doesn't, which is helping people figure out a way to treat each other well."[3] How much do you agree or disagree with his critique of religion's effectiveness at teaching us to forgive and treat one another well? Why?

"I Doubt It" (reprise)

15. Thomas's meeting with the risen Jesus in *Easter Mysteries* closely follows **John 20:24-29** (though it compresses Thomas's absence for dramatic purposes):

   > Thomas, the one called Didymus, one of the Twelve, wasn't with the disciples when Jesus came. The other disciples told him, "We've seen the Lord!"
   >
   > But he replied, "Unless I see the nail marks in his hands, put my finger in the wounds left by the nails, and put my hand into his side, I won't believe."
   >
   > After eight days his disciples were again in a house and Thomas was with them. Even though the doors were locked, Jesus entered and stood among them. He said, "Peace be with you." Then he said to Thomas, "Put your finger here. Look at my hands. Put your hand into my side. No more disbelief. Believe!"
   >
   > Thomas responded to Jesus, "My Lord and my God!"
   >
   > Jesus replied, "Do you believe because you see me? Happy are those who don't see and yet believe."

   Thomas is popularly known, in church and culture, as "Doubting Thomas." How fairly do you think the nickname applies? Read **John 11:1-16** (alluded to in Scene 11 of *Easter Mysteries*). How does Thomas's behavior in

Ascension

If there's a hungry child before you,
Feed the hungry child before you
And you'll feel my presence tremble in the air.
Seek out a stranger and befriend him,
Lacking justice, then defend him.
You may notice when you do these things, I'm there.
I am never far away. If you'd truly wish I'd stay,
If it's close you want to be, follow me.

Don't leave your ailing friend that's dying.
It's on you that I'm relying.
You should know that you can find me anywhere.
There's not a prison that's not lonely,
Full of prisoners that only
Live a solitude that's shattered with despair.
I am never far away . . .

John 11 shape your opinion of him in John 20? Why does Jesus offer to let Thomas touch him as Thomas said he wanted to, and why does Thomas not follow through? How are "those who don't see [Jesus] and yet believe" "happy" (CEB) or "blessed" (NRSV)?

16. In *Easter Mysteries*, Jesus briefly chuckles as he greets Thomas. Why do you suppose he made this choice? Do you like how the actors play this encounter? Why or why not?

"Follow Me"

17. While Jesus's last scene in *Easter Mysteries* draws on some details from Luke's accounts of the Ascension (**Luke 24:49-53; Acts 1:8-11**) and on Matthew's account of Jesus's Great Commission (**Matthew 28:16-20**), it most closely resembles Jesus's words about his coming again in glory in **Matthew 25:31-40**:

> "Now when the Human One comes in his majesty and all his angels are with him, he will sit on his majestic throne. All the nations will be gathered in front of him. He will separate them from each other, just as a shepherd separates the sheep from the goats. He will put the sheep on his right side. But the goats he will put on his left.
>
> "Then the king will say to those on his right, 'Come, you who will receive good things from my Father. Inherit the kingdom that was prepared for you before the world

Mission

began. I was hungry and you gave me food to eat. I was thirsty and you gave me a drink. I was a stranger and you welcomed me. I was naked and you gave me clothes to wear. I was sick and you took care of me. I was in prison and you visited me.'

"Then those who are righteous will reply to him, 'Lord, when did we see you hungry and feed you, or thirsty and give you a drink? When did we see you as a stranger and welcome you, or naked and give you clothes to wear? When did we see you sick or in prison and visit you?'

"Then the king will reply to them, 'I assure you that when you have done it for one of the least of these brothers and sisters of mine, you have done it for me.'"

Commenting on Jesus's final song in *Easter Mysteries*, Henry Rietz writes:

> Here the theology of Matthew is changed from Jesus being the person in need, to the follower who is doing the work of Jesus manifesting the presence of Jesus. With this, [playwright John] O'Boyle provides us with a physical, material ethic—do good to others—that we might emulate and embrace as true, regardless of what we may otherwise think or believe. That is Good News![4]

How do you respond to the song's interpretation of Matthew 25? What connection does

the song make between following Jesus and
"ascending" with him?

> If there's a hungry child before you,
> Feed the hungry child before you
> And you'll feel my presence tremble in the air.
> Seek out a stranger and befriend him,
> Lacking justice, then defend him.
> You may notice when you do these things,
>   I'm there.
> I am never far away. If you'd truly wish I'd stay,
> If it's close you want to be, follow me.
>
> Don't leave your ailing friend that's dying.
> It's on you that I'm relying.
> You should know that you can find me
>   anywhere.
> There's not a prison that's not lonely,
> Full of prisoners that only
> Live a solitude that's shattered with
>   despair.
> I am never far away. If you'd truly wish I'd stay,
> If it's close you want to be, follow me.
>
> I'll never be offended if you walk in my path,
> The all of what you do, you do for me.
> Don't worry that I'll leave you.
> Here's a truth that's sublime,
> I am with you always, yes, until the very
>   end of time.
>
> If there's a man in rags before you,
> Clothe the man in rags before you.

You will find your robe is large enough for two.
To quench a thirst when giving water
Give them also living water.
You will find abundant water there for you.
I am never far away. If you'd truly wish I'd stay,
If it's close you want to be, ascend with me.[5]

Finale—"Oh, Spirit Come" and "Now Comes the Dawn" (reprise)

Oh, Spirit come! Come to me now!
Bring forth your light! Bring forth your love!
Rise like the sun, burst from the sea!
Spill forth your pow'r, pour over me!

Quick, turn and come back before my
  hopes fade!
Don't waste a moment, don't leave me
  afraid!

Oh, Spirit come! Be by my side!
Be on my lips! Be in my life!
Circles of fire burn over me,
Kindle my heart, set my flame free!
Teach me to sing, right every wrong.
Please help me now, please teach me how.
Let me be your song.[6]

18. Why do you think the song after Jesus's ascension bears such a strong similarity to the three women's song from Scene 11, in which they reported their discovery of Jesus's empty

tomb? In what important way does this song differ from the earlier song, and why?

19. What does the staging of this song suggest to you about the coming of the Holy Spirit and the Spirit's effect on Jesus's followers?

20. What images do Jesus's followers use to describe the Holy Spirit in this song? Which of these images speaks most powerfully to you, and why? When you picture the Holy Spirit, what images do you see in your mind's eye and in your heart?

21. According to John O'Boyle, the first draft of *Easter Mysteries* ended with the disciples' prayer for the Holy Spirit. How would you have reacted had the show ended at this point? Why do you think O'Boyle decided to end the show as it currently ends?

22. How does Mary Magdalene help the rest of Jesus's followers find resolve and hope at the close of the show? What do her words and actions at this moment suggest about how Christians can be for each other, and for the world, an answer to prayers for the Holy Spirit's presence?

23. What can you infer from the final number about whether and how Mary Magdalene and Peter now relate to each other? What lessons can people in the church who may be at odds with one another draw from the way *Easter Mysteries* depicts these two key figures' relationship?

Mission

24. As *Easter Mysteries* ends, the cast sings:

> *This is the dawn*
> *When all the dreams you ever dreamed*
> *Could now come true.*
> *There's nothing stopping them for you.*
> *You're now awake, so you can live them all,*
> *And bigger dreams you never dreamed,*
> *They also will come true.*[7]

In what ways is the church today called to dream and to live out "bigger dreams"? How do we know when our dreams are the dreams from God promised at the first Christian Pentecost (**Acts 2:17**)? What does it look like for the individual believer and the community of faith to be truly "awake"?

MUSIC

As Easter begins to come, the cast sings:

> This is the Light
> When all the dreams you ever dreamed
> Could had come true.
> That is, nothing happens that is you.
> You've not needed to, or came to them all,
> And hopes so apt you never dreamed of
> That also will come true.

What wave is the church today! afted to beath another what! hagar d.e.a.r.?" How do we know what our dreams are the d.e.a.ns from looking in used at the truth, what quite reco. (Acts 24:12) What does it look like ?! The individual believer and the Communally of faith are truly aware."

♪

Leader Helps

Suggested Screening Schedule

With a running time of just under 90 minutes, *Easter Mysteries* is an ideal length for a group or even congregational "movie night" (or, if preferred, a matinee!).

A schedule for such an event might look like this:

6:00 p.m.–6:30 p.m.	Communal meal
6:30 p.m.–8:00 p.m.	Watch *Easter Mysteries*
8:00 p.m.–8:30 p.m.	Discussion
8:30 p.m.–8:45 p.m	Brief closing worship (hymn, prayer, Holy Communion)

You could lead your screening in someone's home or at your church building, especially if you wish to invite neighbors from the community to attend. Be sure to arrange a space with adequate and comfortable seating, and a screen large enough for everyone to easily see. Be sure to test your video, audio, and internet streaming connection just before your event begins, so you are confident everything is in working order.

Although the film is titled *Easter Mysteries*, its emphasis on the nature of a community of faith makes it appropriate for any time of year.

Additionally, note that *Easter Mysteries* has appealed to audiences from non-Christian backgrounds as well as Christian ones. You could use the film as a basis for an interfaith gathering (in which case you will want to carefully plan any worship elements in your event), or as a nonthreatening event to which your members can invite their non-Christian family, friends, and neighbors to attend (in which case you may want to leave out any worship elements).

You might also consider making *Easter Mysteries* a double feature with some other film as a daylong "mini-retreat" for your congregation. (For example: In 2018, *Easter Mysteries* aired on NBC on Easter Sunday, as did the network's live production of *Jesus Christ Superstar*, which is available on DVD. Comparing and contrasting the two films' approach to the same story could prove interesting and could provoke fresh insights into the Easter story for participants.)

Suggested Discussion Prompts

When watching *Easter Mysteries* in a single session, a group will not have time to work its way through all or even most of the questions provided in Sessions 1–3. As leader, you should read those questions and plan to ask any that seem especially appropriate to your group; however, you will need

Leader Helps

to facilitate a discussion largely based on viewers' immediate reactions to the pieces as a whole, and on its broad, overarching themes.

Before you begin the screening portion of your event, invite participants to say something about why they are interested in seeing and discussing *Easter Mysteries*. Tell the group of your own interest, and express excitement about your time together.

Ask:

- What does the title of the production we are about to watch, *Easter Mysteries*, lead you to expect from it?
- What "mysteries" connected with or questions about the Easter story have you had, or do you have today?

You may wish to write people's questions on newsprint or marker board for ease of reference, and may need to prompt group participation by first asking some questions of your own. Assure participants there are no wrong, stupid, or bad questions. Tell them not to rush to answer someone else's question. This exercise is simply a chance to ask questions about a story familiar to most Christians—and, because of Christianity's historic and cultural influence, to many non-Christians as well. Encourage participants to keep these questions in mind as they watch the film, and to make mental notes of other questions watching the film raises for them.

Leader Helps

If desired (and appropriate, considering your participants), lead the group in a prayer like that provided for Session 1 before beginning the film.

After the film, use some or all of these questions to facilitate discussion:

- How is *Easter Mysteries* like and unlike other dramatizations of the Easter story you are familiar with?
- What did you like most and like least about *Easter Mysteries*, and why?
- John O'Boyle, the author of *Easter Mysteries*, has said he wanted to write a play that "de-iconized" the story's famous characters in order to make them more relatable. Do you think he succeeded? Why or why not? Which character could you identify or empathize with the most? The least? Why?
- What do you think *Easter Mysteries* has to say about the meaning and importance of Jesus's death and resurrection?
- Peter is arguably the main protagonist in *Easter Mysteries*. What is Peter's central struggle in the play? What obstacles keep him for achieving his goal(s), and how does he overcome them? How does viewing the Easter story primarily from Peter's point of view influence what you think, feel, and believe about it?
- Mary Magdalene is a key character in *Easter Mysteries*. What is her struggle in the show, and how does she overcome it? How does

the attention the show pays to her influence your perspective on the Easter story?
- What practical lessons do you think people today might learn from *Easter Mysteries* about what it means to live as a community of faith? About what it means to live an authentically human life?

Notes

Foreword

1. Quoted by A. James Rudin, "Christians, Jews and the Dubious History of the Passion Play," Religion News Service, March 27, 2018, https://religionnews.com/2018/03/27/christians-jews-and-the-dubious-history-of-the-passion-play/.
2. Lewis Segal, "Oberammergau Passion Play Is a Changing Tradition," *Los Angeles Times*, August 15, 2010, www.latimes.com/archives/la-xpm-2010-aug-15-la-ca-oberammergau-20100815-story.html.
3. Sr. Rose Pacatte, "A Decade Later, 'The Passion' Still Raises Questions of Anti-Semitism," *National Catholic Reporter*, February 22, 2014, www.ncronline.org/news/media/decade-later-passion-still-raises-questions-anti-semitism.
4. John O'Boyle, "Easter Mysteries Creatives 1," May 11, 2019, https://vimeo.com/335609105.
5. Charles Runnells, "Written by Naples Man, Easter Movie Musical Goes National," *News-Press* (Fort Myers, FL), March 20, 2016, www.news-press.com/story/entertainment/2016/03/20/written-naples-man-easter-movie-musical-goes-national/81917840/.
6. Nell Minow, "Interview: John O'Boyle on the Easter Mysteries Musical," March 15, 2016, https://moviemom.com/interview-john-oboyle-on-the-easter-mysteries-musical/.

Notes

7. Rudin, "Christians, Jews."
8. John O'Boyle, "EM Series Ep 7 Humanizing Icons 1.5," April 23, 2019, https://vimeo.com/332053906.
9. Minow, "Interview: John O'Boyle."
10. John O'Boyle, "EM Series Ep 3 Transcending Religion," April 23, 2019, https://vimeo.com/332053509.
11. O'Boyle, "Transcending Religion."
12. O'Boyle, "EM Series Ep 7 Humanizing Icons."
13. John O'Boyle, "Easter Mysteries—Behind the Scenes Series 'Hope and Love,'" April 23, 2019, https://vimeo.com/332053963.

Session 1: Passion

1. John O'Boyle, "This Is My Body," *Easter Mysteries* video (0:10:19–0:11:30).
2. Henry Rietz, "Remembering and Embodying: John O'Boyle's *Easter Mysteries*," Grinnell College, April 11, 2019.
3. John O'Boyle, "Gethsemane," *Easter Mysteries* video (0:13:35–0:15:27).
4. John O'Boyle, "Wash My Hands," *Easter Mysteries* video (0:19:41–0:24:32).
5. John O'Boyle, "Requiem," *Easter Mysteries* video (0:33:41–0:35:25).

Session 2: Resurrection

1. For more information, see "Liturgical Drama," *Encyclopedia Britannica*, www.britannica.com/topic/liturgical-drama; "Quem Quaeritis"—Early English Drama (Princeton, NJ: Films for the Humanities, 1975), www.youtube.com/watch?v=fJmSalBklTI; "The Death and Resurrection of Theater as . . .

Notes

Liturgical Drama: Crash Course Theater #8," April 6, 2018, www.youtube.com/watch?v=kX0jHv05FYM.
2. Henry Rietz, "Remembering and Embodying: John O'Boyle's *Easter Mysteries*," Grinnell College, April 11, 2019.
3. John O'Boyle, "I Will Wipe Away Each Tear," *Easter Mysteries* video (0:57:48–0:59:58).

Session 3: Mission

1. John O'Boyle, "On the Road to Emmaus," *Easter Mysteries* video (1:01:48–1:02:06).
2. John O'Boyle, *Easter Mysteries*, https://vimeo.com/336215295, at about the 00:00:33 mark.
3. John O'Boyle, "Easter Mysteries—Behind the Scenes Series 'Forgiveness,'" https://vimeo.com/332053983.
4. Henry Rietz, "Remembering and Embodying: John O'Boyle's *Easter Mysteries*," Grinnell College, April 11, 2019.
5. John O'Boyle, "Ascension," *Easter Mysteries* video (1:18:20–1:20:32).
6. John O'Boyle, "Finale," *Easter Mysteries* video (1:22:54–1:24:10).
7. O'Boyle, "Finale" (1:26:02–1:26:34).